Letort Paper

UNDERSTANDING THE NORTH KOREA PROBLEM: WHY IT HAS BECOME THE "LAND OF LOUSY OPTIONS"

William Boik

July 2011

The views expressed in this report are those of the author and do not necessarily reflect the official policy or position of the Department of the Army, the Department of Defense, or the U.S. Government. Authors of Strategic Studies Institute (SSI) publications enjoy full academic freedom, provided they do not disclose classified information, jeopardize operations security, or misrepresent official U.S. policy. Such academic freedom empowers them to offer new and sometimes controversial perspectives in the interest of furthering debate on key issues. This report is cleared for public release; distribution is unlimited.

*****

*****

Comments pertaining to this report are invited and should be forwarded to: Director, Strategic Studies Institute, U.S. Army War College, 632 Wright Ave, Carlisle, PA 17013-5046.

*****

All Strategic Studies Institute (SSI) publications may be downloaded free of charge from the SSI website. Hard copies of this report may also be obtained free of charge while supplies last by placing an order on the SSI website. The SSI website address is: *www.StrategicStudiesInstitute.army.mil*.

*****

The Strategic Studies Institute publishes a monthly e-mail newsletter to update the national security community on the research of our analysts, recent and forthcoming publications, and upcoming conferences sponsored by the Institute. Each newsletter also provides a strategic commentary by one of our research analysts. If you are interested in receiving this newsletter, please subscribe on the SSI website at *www.StrategicStudiesInstitute. army.mil/newsletter/*.

FOREWORD

This monograph is intended to draw attention to the challenges faced by the United States in developing a coordinated strategy for dealing with North Korea. Despite the many decades of direct U.S. involvement on the Korean Peninsula, we continue to have little understanding of the North Korean culture or of events inside North Korea. We also do not have a long-term coordinated strategy for North Korea. Over the past decade, the United States has focused much of its attention on the Middle East and the War on Terror, and seems to only focus on North Korea in response to crises when they arise on the peninsula.

Mr. Boik provides a timely analysis and thoughtful insights into the significant challenges faced by the United States in developing a strategy for North Korea. He examines the complex history of U.S. policy toward North Korea over the past decade that has left the United States in a position of having no real strategy and virtually no influence over North Korea. He accurately addresses the complicated regional concerns and national security interests of North Korea's neighbors and their impact on each country's approach to North Korea. Most importantly, he looks at how the North Korean culture and history have influenced the attitudes of North Korean society and their relationship with the outside world. He concludes by pointing out that, despite the numerous inherent challenges, the United States must develop a strategy to engage Pyongyang if we expect to have any influence over the future direction of events in North Korea.

Mr. Boik is uniquely qualified to write this analysis, having served as the Senior U.S. Government Representative in Pyongyang, North Korea, during two 30-day Joint U.S.-Democratic People's Republic of Korea (North Korea) Missing-in-Action (MIA) Recovery Operations, which searched for missing American soldiers from the Korean War. In this position, he was able to travel throughout North Korea and had daily contact with senior North Korean military and foreign ministry officials. Additionally, Mr. Boik has participated as a member of a Department of Defense delegation negotiating access to North Korean sites for the MIA recovery teams.

The Strategic Studies Institute is pleased to offer this monograph as a contribution to the national security debate on North Korea. This analysis should be especially useful to U.S. strategic leaders and intelligence professionals as they seek to address the complicated factors related to U.S. policy toward the Korean Peninsula. This work will also benefit those seeking a greater understanding of the policy issues related to North Korea.

DOUGLAS C. LOVELACE, JR.
Director
Strategic Studies Institute

ABOUT THE AUTHOR

BILL BOIK is a senior civilian staff member in the Defense Prisoner of War/Missing Personnel Office. He retired from the U.S. Army as a Colonel in 2005 after 30 years of active and reserve service. During his career, he served in various Armor and Military Intelligence positions in South Korea, the United States, and Germany. He led two separate Joint Missing in Action (MIA) Recovery Teams to the Democratic People's Republic of Korea (North Korea) from September-October 2001 and July-August 2002 in search of missing U.S. servicemen from the Korean Conflict. While in North Korea, he served as the Senior U.S. Government Official in Pyongyang during each of these month-long recovery operations. Colonel Boik is the author of *Orders, Decorations, and Medals of the Democratic People's Republic of Korea* (2008). Colonel Boik holds a Master of Arts Degree in Strategic Security Studies from the National Defense University, a Master of Arts Degree in International Relations from Boston University, and a Master of Science Degree in Strategic Intelligence from the Defense Intelligence College.

SUMMARY

This monograph is intended to generate discussion on the challenges of developing a coordinated U.S. strategy toward North Korea. It begins by looking at U.S. policy and actions toward North Korea and the situation on the Korean Peninsula over the past decade. This monograph examines the regional interests of China, Russia, South Korea, Japan, and the United States in relation to North Korea and the impact that North Korean culture and traditions have had on North Korean society.

Based on this analysis, the monograph recommends that, if we expect to have any influence over events in North Korea, U.S. policy must emphasize engagement with Pyongyang. This engagement should include discussions, negotiations, cultural exchanges, and even diplomatic relations. Only by engaging North Korea on multiple levels, will we begin to understand each other, and only then will we be able to exercise some level of positive influence on them.

This will not be easy, nor will it happen quickly. North Korea is a difficult nation to negotiate with and often reacts in a manner that outside observers see as counterproductive. Although it will not be easy, a policy of actively engaging North Korea will eventually provide the United States with a forum to exert a limited degree of influence on the Pyongyang leadership. It will also give us a better understanding of what is actually happening inside North Korea. Ultimately, we must keep in mind that, as in the case of Eastern Europe, events on the ground are likely to outpace any planning we do. It is extremely critical that we have both an awareness of events as they are occurring and the flexibility of action to ensure appropriate measured responses.

A policy of engagement toward the North is also a double-edged sword for the Pyongyang leadership. North Korea's biggest weakness may, in fact, be opening up to the West. When this begins to happen, there is significant potential for the regime to be weakened. Yet North Korea's current economic situation leaves its leadership few options. The leadership seems to understand that they must work with the United States and other nations in order to get assistance. However, the more North Korea's population is able to see and have contact with Americans and other Westerners, the more they will start to see what they really do not have and cannot achieve under the current regime. The challenge will then become one of controlling the North Korean population's expectations and grievances so they do not resort to violence.

Map 1. Democratic People's Republic of Korea (North Korea).

	North Korea	South Korea
Total Area	120,540 sq km	98,480 sq km
Land	120,410 sq km	98,190 sq km
Water	130 sq km	290 sq km
Land Use		
Arable Land	22.40%	16.58%
Permanent Crops	1.66%	2.01%
Other	75.94%	81.41% (2005)
People		
Population	23,479,088 (July 2008 est.)	48,379,392 (July 2008 est.)
Age Structure		
0-14 Yrs Old	22.9% (male 2,733,352 female 2,654,186)	17.4% (male 4,431,315 female 4,004,810)
15-64 Yrs Old	68.2% (male 7,931,484 female 8,083,626)	72% (male 17,760,975 female 17,095,436)
Over 65 Yrs Old	8.8% (make 751,401 female 1,325,040)	10.5% (male 2,030,931 female 3,055,925)
Median Age	32.7	36.7
Population Growth Rate	0.73%	0.27%
Literacy Rate	99.90%	97.90%
Economy		
GDP	$40 billion	$1,312 trillion
GDP Growth Rate	1.10%	4.30%
GDP Per Capita	$1,800	$27,100
GDP by Sector	Agriculture 23.3% Industry 43.1% Services 33.6%	Agriculture 2.9% Industry 39.4% Services 57.7%
Labor Force	20 Million (2004 est)	24.34 Million
Unemployment Rate	na	3.20%
Transportation		
Railways	5,235 std guage	3,381 std guage
Roadways	724 km paved 24,830 km unpaved	83,640 km paved 23,000 km unpaved
Military		
Manpower	1.1 million (4.7 Reserves) (2005 est)	687,700
Military Expenditure	$5.1 billion (31% GDP)(2005 est)	$14.5 billion(2.7% GDP)

Note: Adapted from the *CIA World Factbook 2009*, New York: Skyhorse Publishing Co. Ltd., 2008.

Figure 1. Comparison between North and South Korea.

CHAPTER 1

INTRODUCTION

Few conflicts are as protracted as the one in Korea, where deeply hostile and anachronistic Cold War attitudes have posed major security problems for half a century. To be more precise, two specters haunt the peninsula: a military escalation, even outright war, and a North Korean collapse, which could easily destabilize the northeast Asian region.

> Roland Bleiker
> Author of "Divided North Korea:
> Toward a Culture of Reconciliation"[1]

For more than 20 years, the Democratic People's Republic of Korea (North Korea, or DPRK) has been a problem for various U.S. policymakers. During the 1990s, North Korea faced several crises. In 1991, the Soviet Union, its key ally, collapsed, ending the main source of financial support for the regime. Three years later in 1994, the "Great Leader," Kim Il Sung, died. In the mid-to-late 1990s, North Korea faced severe flooding and famine. To many observers, it appeared that North Korea had little chance of survival, and that the country would collapse within a few years.

Today, however, as a result of missed opportunities, the United States finds itself faced with a North Korea that has a limited nuclear capability it is unlikely to be willing to negotiate away. On January 15, 2009, the *London Times* reported that Kim Jong Il had finally designated his youngest son, 25-year-old Kim Jong Un, as his successor.[2] Little is known about Kim Jong Un in the West beyond the fact that he was educated in Switzerland. He has seldom been seen in public. More importantly, it appears that unlike the efforts made by Kim Il Sung to groom Kim Jong Il to assume power, little has been done to prepare Kim Jong Un or the North Korean people for this succession, making it unclear whether the central government in Pyongyang will be able to maintain stability once Kim Jong Il dies.

Perhaps the most critical challenge for the United States is that our current strategy for dealing with North Korea continues to be reactive and focused almost exclusively on the issue of nuclear weapons. U.S. policymakers appear to have made little or no effort to develop a broader regional strategy for dealing with events in North Korea once Kim Jong Il dies. There also appears to be little effort being made to put the United States in a position to influence events that could bring about a peaceful unification of the two Koreas. As Victor Cha, Director of Asian Studies, Georgetown University, recently wrote, "In what would be the single most important contingency that could impact the South Korean economy and security for decades, there is no agreed upon plan for how to deal with a collapsing North Korea."[3] He further wrote,

> Given the stakes involved, you would think that the U.S., South Korea and other regional partners had some type of agreed upon plan. Nope. There is a "concept plan" that has been discussed in the past between Washington and Seoul, but all dialogue ceased under the previous administration in Seoul. The Roh Moohyun government rejected planning discussions because it believed that such discussions would offend Pyongyang and give the impression that the U.S. and Seoul were actively conspiring to collapse the regime. The Roh government instead tried to work on its own plan, without sharing any common concept of operations with the U.S. [4]

Sadly, it appears that the U.S. Government also failed to capitalize on President Clinton's recent mission to North Korea. While he successfully obtained the release of two U.S. journalists being held by North Korea, it does not appear that any opportunities to move forward were discussed, despite the fact that he was the first senior American to meet with Kim Jong Il since Ambassador Madeleine Albright's visit almost a decade ago.

Incredibly little is actually known about the North Korean leadership and events inside the country. Few Westerners and almost no Americans have been allowed to visit North Korea in recent years, leading to an incomplete understanding of the North. That is our greatest challenge in developing any strategy for the Korean Peninsula.

ENDNOTES - CHAPTER 1

1. Roland Bleiker, *Divided Korea: Toward a Culture of Reconciliation*, Minneapolis, MN: University of Minnesota Press, 2005, p. ix.

2. Leo Lewis, "Kim Jong Il 'Names Favourite Son Jong Un as Successor' in North Korea," *London Times,* January 15, 2009, available from *www.prisonplanet.comkim-jong-il-names-favourite-son-jong-un-as-successor-in-north-korea.html*.

3. Victor Cha, "We Have No Plan," *Chosun Ilbo,* June 9, 2008, available from *english.chosun.com/w21data/html/news/200806/2008 06090015.html*.

4. *Ibid.*

CHAPTER 2

PUTTING THE KOREAN PENINSULA IN CONTEXT

The question (preparing for a collapse of the North Korean regime) has been completely taboo. The major players are completely unprepared. The South Koreans don't want to touch it, and the U.S. takes its lead from the South.

Andrei Lankov
(North Korea Expert)
Kookmin University (Seoul)[1]

INTRODUCTION

This chapter will address the situation on the Korean Peninsula from the perspective of recent U.S. policy and actions toward North Korea. It will look at North Korea from the overall context of the international environment and it will address the first component of the Interagency Conflict Management Strategy Model[2] considerations by defining the problem and providing an assessment of the current situation in North Korea and on the peninsula. Finally, the chapter will look at the nature of the threat posed by North Korea.

BACKGROUND

Throughout most of the last 10 years, critics have argued that the United States under President Bush seemed to have little interest or inclination in developing a coherent policy for engaging North Korea. In fact, until the last few years of the Bush administration, it appears that the accepted approach toward North

Korea was simply to have no meaningful contact at all with Pyongyang. This apparent lack of a coherent policy approach only served to limit further the U.S. ability to influence events both in North Korea and on the Korean Peninsula.

For much of the Bush administration, it could be argued that U.S. actions were focused almost exclusively on isolating North Korea (both diplomatically and economically) in an effort to prevent the Pyongyang regime from developing a nuclear capability. The administration's policy had four major elements:

1. An immediate North Korean commitment to dismantle nuclear weapons facilities;

2. No direct negotiations until North Korea dismantled all nuclear weapons facilities;

3. Isolation of North Korea through economic sanctions; and,

4. Encouraging regime change in North Korea.[3]

The Bush administration seemed to feel that simply by isolating North Korea and refusing to negotiate in any meaningful way, the Pyongyang regime would eventually come to its senses and give up its nuclear ambitions.

Unfortunately, this strategy of emphasizing isolation over meaningful engagement with Pyongyang only played into the hands of the North Korean leadership. First, North Korea was, and currently remains, one of the most isolated countries in the world, by its own leadership's choice. There has been virtually nothing the United States could do to further isolate the country. In fact, this policy of nonengagement only made it easier for the Pyongyang regime to keep its people isolated and cut off from the outside world.

Second, U.S. calls for military action aimed at regime change only made it easier for the North Korean propaganda machine to emphasize U.S. aggressive and potentially threatening actions. This, in turn, made it even more important for the Korean People's Army (KPA, or the North Korean Army) to be ready to repel an invasion. Finally, U.S. calls for regime change in Pyongyang and discussion of the North Korean people's desire for democracy showed a failure by U.S. policymakers to understand the nature of the North Korean people and North Korean leadership.

DEFINING THE UNITED STATES POLICY GOAL

While the basic U.S. policy goal for the region has been peace, security, and stability on the Korean Peninsula, each U.S. presidential administration has defined this goal in its own way. In 2000, the final Clinton administration *National Security Strategy* (NSS) stated, "We must enhance cooperation with South Korea as we encourage North Korea's emergence from isolation and continue to diminish the missile threat."[4] It also devoted a whole section to a detailed U.S. strategy for the Korean Peninsula and support for reunification of the two Koreas.

In 2002, the Bush administration's first NSS approached the Korean issue from a different perspective. It emphasized the threat posed by North Korea's weapons proliferation and nuclear development activities. The strategy also emphasized working with South Korea to contribute to broader security in the region and overall stability on the Korean Peninsula.[5] In 2006, the final Bush administration NSS focused on ending tyranny in North Korea; ending the threat it posed with its nuclear weapons development program; and on sharing South Korea's vision of a prosperous, democratic, and united Korean Peninsula.[6]

THE BUSH ADMINISTRATION AND NORTH KOREA

The Bush administration entered office in 2001 convinced that the Clinton administration had given too much to North Korea in the 1994 Agreed Framework without ensuring a verifiable reduction of the threat posed by its nuclear weapons development program.[7] As a result, upon assuming office, President Bush ordered an immediate halt to all high-level U.S. Government contacts with North Korea. He also called for a complete review of U.S. policy toward North Korea at the same time. In effect, all movement on the 1994 Agreed Framework and all official U.S. Government contact with North Korea was stopped, pending the administration's review of the policy. South Korean President Kim Dae Jung was also told that the United States would no longer support his ongoing reconciliation efforts with North Korea.

President Bush announced completion of the policy review on June 6, 2001. The new U.S. policy called for a "comprehensive approach," addressing verifiable constraints on North Korean missile development, less-threatening conventional forces, and improved human rights conditions in North Korea.[8] The new approach, however, required North Korea to take serious steps to improve relations with the United States first. Then and only then would the United States move forward with any new initiatives. However, North Korea was not seen as a high priority for the Bush administration. The War on Terrorism and events in Afghanistan and Iraq were more critical to

U.S. security. Essentially, President Bush and his advisors seemed to feel that it was easier to simply wait North Korea out than deal with Pyongyang directly.

Between 2001 and 2002, there was virtually no official U.S. Government contact with North Korea other than through the Defense Prisoner of War/Missing Personnel Office (DPMO). This office was negotiating for access to U.S. Korean War loss sites in North Korea and conducting limited remains-recovery operations inside North Korea.[9]

Throughout 2001, U.S. contact with North Korea continued to deteriorate. Following September 11, 2001 (9/11), President Bush included North Korea along with Iran and Iraq as part of the "axis of evil" in his 2002 State of the Union speech. While this might have made good imagery for the American public recovering from the 9/11 attacks, it had serious consequences for the administration's efforts to influence events on the Korean Peninsula. Not only did the idea of North Korea being part of the "axis of evil" further raise concerns in North Korea that the United States ultimately intended to attack; it also complicated South Korea's relationship with North. It also tied the hands of the United States in terms of any movement forward on relations with the North. This speech was followed with the release of the first Bush administration NSS in September 2002. This document emphasized pre-emptive action against rogue states and mentioned both Iraq and North Korea by name.

Between 2001 and 2006, U.S. policy toward North Korea focused on isolating the regime and eliminating the North Korean nuclear weapons program. Specifically, the policy called for: [10]

1. Diplomatic engagement with North Korea through regional discussions;

2. Nonproliferation of technology or weapons by North Korea;

3. Reduction or elimination of trafficking by North Korea of illegal drugs, counterfeit currency, and other contraband;

4. Maintaining U.S. military forces in South Korea and Japan as a credible military deterrent to North Korean aggression;

5. Implementing fully the UN sanctions to penalize and isolate the North Korean regime;

6. Keeping North Korea on the list of terrorist/terrorist-supporter states; and,

7. Continuing to keep North Korea from becoming a member of international financial institutions.

As a result of this policy, few actions were taken by the Bush administration to reduce tensions on the Korean Peninsula, and virtually no official U.S. Government contact occurred between the United States and North Korea. As tension with North Korea continued to increase, the Bush administration made its first high-level contact with North Korea in October 2002 when Undersecretary of State James Kelly traveled to Pyongyang in order to discuss North Korean weapons of mass destruction (WMD) development, arms exports, and human rights issues. During the meeting, Kelly accused North Korea of having an enriched uranium program and later claimed that the North Koreans admitted to it when he made the charge.[11] Although the North Korean government claimed that it only stated that as a sovereign state it had the right to have nuclear weapons, the situation continued to deteriorate.

By mid-October 2002, senior administration officials were calling the 1994 Agreed Framework dead, and in November, the United States reached an agreement with South Korea and Japan to suspend the heavy-fuel-oil deliveries to North Korea that were required by the 1994 Agreed Framework. Shortly after this action, North Korea declared that the Agreed Framework had collapsed and that resulting energy shortages had forced it to restart operations at the country's nuclear facilities, which had been closed in 1994. In December 2003, North Korea requested that the International Atomic Energy Agency (IAEA) remove its locks and cameras from declared nuclear facilities and announced that it intended to expel the IAEA inspectors by the end of the year. On January 10, 2003, North Korea announced that it was withdrawing from the Nuclear Proliferation Treaty (NPT).

As the standoff worsened, China began taking steps to bring the countries together. The so-called Six-Party Talks, consisting of China, Japan, Russia, South Korea, North Korea, and the United States, were agreed to in 2003. The first round of these talks was held in Beijing, China, in August 2003. However, little progress was made during the initial talks. Four more rounds of talks took place between 2003 and July 2005, when they became totally deadlocked over the nuclear weapons development issue. As a result, no further meetings were held in 2005 or 2006.

On July 4, 2006, North Korea test fired several missiles, one of which was believed to be a Taepo Dong 2.[12] Although the flight appeared to have been terminated due to a problem, North Korea had made the point to the world that it was moving forward with its missile development program. Then, on October 9, 2006, North Korea announced that it had conducted an underground test of a nuclear weapon. This test was confirmed several days later by U.S. intelligence, which believed the size of the explosion to be less than 1 kiloton (kt).[13]

Figure 2-1 shows a graphic example of the range capabilities of the various North Korean missiles. Most significant is the fact that, the North Korean Taepo Dong 2 is capable of reaching Alaska and the continental United States.

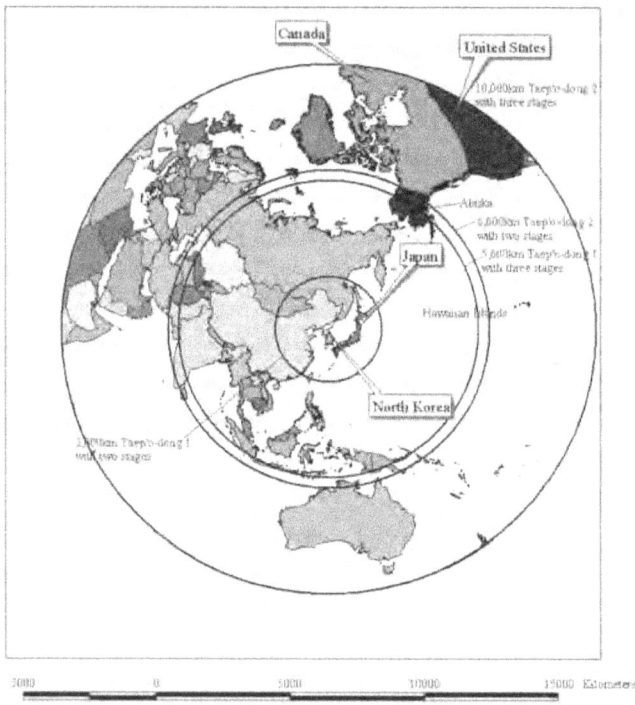

Note: North Korean Advisory Group Report to the Speaker of the House of Representatives. Available from *www.house.gov/ international_relations/nkag/report.htm.*

Figure 2-1. Potential North Korean Long-Range Missile Capabilities.

By early 2007, China was making a renewed push to restart the Six-Party Talks. By this time, the Republican Party had suffered a major defeat in the 2006 congressional elections, and there was a new national security team, with a new Secretary of State, Secretary of Defense, and National Security Advisor. With this new team, there appeared to be a realization that a shift in policy was needed. The U.S. negotiator with North Korea, Ambassador Christopher Hill, returned to Beijing with a more open attitude and what appeared to be more flexibility. Within a short period, North Korea agreed to dismantle the Yongbyon nuclear facility, allow IAEA inspections, and provide information on its nuclear programs. In return, the United States agreed to begin bilateral talks with North Korea aimed at moving toward eventual establishment of diplomatic relations with North Korea, removal of North Korea from the list of states sponsoring terrorism, ending trade restrictions, and providing energy assistance.

Despite several delays in the process, North Korea did finally shut down and destroy the reactor at Yongbyon on June 28, 2008. It also eventually provided a large amount of information on its nuclear programs. The United States removed North Korea from the list of nations sponsoring terrorism, provided limited energy and food assistance, and began the process of lifting trade restrictions. However, following Kim Jong Il's apparent stroke in August 2008 and the change in governments in both Seoul and Washington at the end of 2008, North Korea has again returned to a hard line and is resisting IAEA inspections and threatening renewed missile and weapons tests.

NORTH KOREA

Most North Koreans have known only two leaders in their lives. The first is Kim Il Sung (see Figure 2.2), the "Great Leader," who is credited with defeating both the Japanese in World War II and the United States in the Korean War, and thereby liberating their country.[14] To the North Koreans, in a country virtually without religion, he was and remains their "god" and a person who could do no wrong.[15] The second is his son, Kim Jong Il, known as the "Dear Leader," or more recently the "Great General," who is credited with rebuilding Pyongyang as a showcase city. To the North Koreans, he is the "son of god" and their guiding light.[16] North Koreans are taught from a very young age that they owe everything they have to Kim Il Sung and Kim Jong Il.

Note: The Books in the Painting are the Works of Kim Il Sung. (Author's Collection.)

Figure 2-2. North Korean Painting Extolling the Greatness of Kim Il Sung.

According to Scott Snyder of the United States Institute of Peace,

> Perhaps the most unique, pervasive, and — or to the outside observer — incomprehensible aspect of North Korea's socialization process is the all-encompassing role played by Kim Il Sung, who arguably continues to be the ruling figure — the "Eternal President" — in North Korea even after his death. Kim Il Sungism may have more in common with religions than with other communist regimes. And, like many strong faiths, it feeds on a form of aggrieved nationalism. . . . Once said by Kim, it is said forever. Nobody is allowed to change anything. . . . The durability of Kim's cult of personality even after his death is so powerful that it cannot be discarded lightly. . . .[17]

In the end, both North Korea and its leaders have proved to be amazingly resilient. Kim Jong Il shrewdly ensured that the KPA was fed and supported with his "Army First" policy.[18] This focus on taking care of the Army provided him a strong base of support for his power. Additionally, the majority of North Korean generals and senior officers today owe their promotions directly to him. He further consolidated his position by continuing to emphasize the threat posed by the United States and successfully maintained his control over the country despite the numerous economic and social problems.

The North Korean Economy.

Economically, North Korea continues to be affected in four areas: economic reform, periodic food shortages, public infrastructure, and the medical system. In July 2002, Pyongyang began a series of significant economic reforms by cutting government subsidies on certain things and essentially allowing people to start limited private businesses. This economic openness has gradually led to a situation in which some North Korean individuals are becoming increasingly more interested in making money than in working for the state. The economic reforms included the following measures: [19]

1. Official prices and wages were increased to bring them closer to the black market levels. As part of this program, food, fuel and electricity, and public transport prices all increased significantly;

2. Wage levels were raised to meet increased prices, with soldiers, miners, and scientists receiving the largest increase;

3. Land was de-collectivized, with farmers having the right to sell excess produce;

4. The North Korean *won* was devalued from its artificially high rate of 2.15 to the U.S. dollar to 150 North Korean *won* to the U.S. dollar;

5. Managerial decisions for industry and agriculture were removed from the political decisionmaking process;

6. Government subsidies were cut, and hard budget constraints imposed on enterprises. Enterprises now had to cover their own expenses; and,

7. All enterprises were authorized to sell their surplus goods on the open market.

North Korea continues to suffer from serious food shortages and periodic natural disasters. Most notably, periodic flooding has further damaged or destroyed the limited food supplies available. A recent report indicated high levels of malnourishment among the population. Food shortages appear to be so severe that some reports indicate that they are starting to impact on the military. Figure 2-3 shows the major areas of malnutrition and food shortages in North Korea, the worst being in the Northeast region of the country.[20] This figure also shows the level of food aid, in thousands of metric tons, the United States has continued to provide to North Korea.

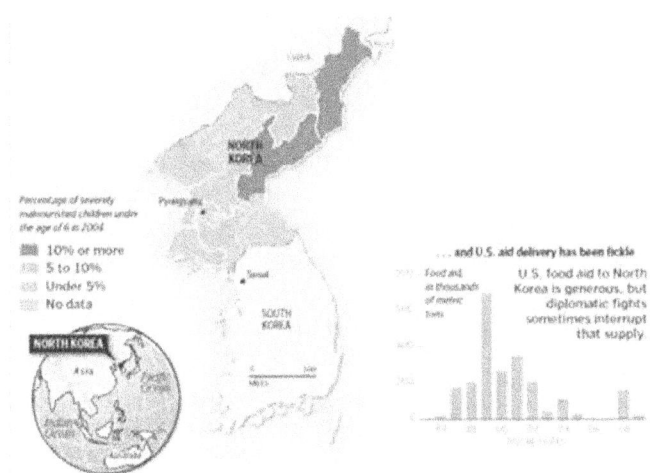

Figure 2-3. Areas of Malnutrition/Food Shortages in North Korea.

The public infrastructure, particularly the condition of railroads, highways, and bridges, is significantly deteriorating, making cross-country transportation difficult. Most factories are not functioning due to aging equipment or they are only functioning on a limited basis due to frequent power outages throughout the country. The North Korean medical system is also nearing collapse, and there are reports of increasing rates of tuberculosis. Medical equipment is old or nonexistent, and medicines are becoming increasingly difficult to obtain. However, the elite in Pyongyang are still able to receive relatively decent medical care.

While there appears to be an awareness of the need for economic reforms by the North Korean leadership, there also appears to be an understanding of the risks posed by too rapid a change. According to Dr. Andrew Scobell,

> North Korea's rulers — or at least some of them — appear to be acutely aware of the dilemma they face. On the one hand, they seem to recognize that, on the surface of it, the most logical way to rescue their economy is to adopt thoroughgoing reforms. On the other hand, they seem to realize that pursuing such a course is likely to mean that they would be undermining their positions in the process — threatening their own power and control. Such reforms might be so successful that after gathering momentum, the regime would eventually find itself reformed out of existence.[21]

Why Is North Korea Developing Nuclear Weapons?

While it is difficult to really know the rationale of the Pyongyang leadership for developing nuclear weapons, much less admitting to having a nuclear weapons program, there are several possible explanations. Their motives seem to stem mostly from a need to have something dramatic that focuses U.S. attention on North Korea. The reasons include:[22]

1. The rapidly deteriorating economic and political situation in the North.

2. The concern by Pyongyang that as part of the "axis of evil" they would be next in line for regime change after Iraq.

3. A possible deliberate action to exploit the anxieties of the United States and its allies about Pyongyang's recklessness by behaving in a manner intended

to exacerbate these apprehensions. Essentially, using the U.S. fear of a possible North Korean nuclear threat to bring about the start of serious negotiations.

A similar analysis comes from a Chinese delegation from the Shanghai Institute during a visit to the University of California (Los Angeles):

> According to the delegates, the admission (of its nuclear development program) is North Korea's way of opening the door for dialogue with the United States. From the North Korean perspective, to develop relations with the United States it is necessary first to get the attention of the United States. North Korea's admission has certainly assured that it (along with Iraq) has moved front-and-center on the foreign policy agenda in Washington. Moreover, North Korea has few cards to play in its relationship with the U.S. North Korea has chosen to play the nuclear card because it wants to reach an understanding—a compromise, in other words—with the United States.[23]

Critics will argue that the North Korean regime is unstable and not capable of coming up with such a long-range plan of action. However, North Korea did successfully manage to refocus U.S. attention on it and saw the Six-Party Talks resume, with the United States taking a more flexible approach. It is important to note that Pyongyang has a record of diplomatic brinkmanship in its dealings with the West. Even in the Department of Defense negotiations for access to possible U.S. missing personnel loss sites in North Korea, the North Korean negotiators will take the discussion to the point of having the talks break down, only to eventually return to the table when they have found the U.S. negotiators' limits. These actions by North Korea would appear to be less the actions of an irrational actor than a deliberate effort to find the U.S. bottom line in an attempt soften the U.S. negotiators and get the most possible from the United States.

To some extent, the North Korean leadership is perhaps a victim of its Cold War negotiating successes. While current situation in the North leaves the country no choice but to negotiate for assistance, North Korea has failed to adapt to these new conditions by modifying its negotiation style. According to Scott Snyder,

> The rigidity of the DPRK's Stalinist institutional structure has inhibited flexibility at the negotiation table and has tied the hands of North Korea's negotiating representatives, who have relatively little authority to make concessions without the direct approval of North Korea's top leadership.[24]

Critics also point to the North Korean WMD development program and its recent missile tests as examples of Pyongyang's direct challenge and threats to the West. However, a closer look at the North Korean program seems to show that North Korea's nuclear weapons development program and recent missile firing may have less to do with preparations to launch an attack (or even to defend themselves) than they do with the Pyongyang regime's efforts to get the attention of the new U.S. President. A recent article by CNN's Christiana Amanpour discusses three possible reasons behind the latest missile launch by Pyongyang. According to her:

> Analysts believe North Korea and its leader Kim Jong-Il conducted the launch for several reasons, including showing off its missile capability to potential buyers, showing off its capability to its own citizens ahead of a rubber-stamp parliamentary session this week in Pyongyang where the leader will be installed again by

acclamation, and finally that Pyongyang conducted the launch as a way of attracting the attention of the Obama administration to focus again on the six-party talks on its nuclear disarmament.[25]

The Threat from North Korea.

As stated above, it appears much of North Korea's efforts in developing nuclear weapons and missiles have been aimed at gaining U.S. attention, rather than developing an offensive capability to launch a war. There appears to be little likelihood that North Korea would use its nuclear or conventional military capability to launch a first-strike attack against the United States or any other nation in the region. The North Korean leadership seems to understand that any attack on the United States or its allies would be suicide and would ultimately destroy the regime, which is the very thing they seek to preserve. According to Dr. Scobell,

> The North Korean leadership probably believes that in any major force-on-force conflict with the United States the Korean People's Army would be defeated, leading to the collapse or overthrow of the regime. The clearest indication of this fear and the existence of this logic in the north is that, for more than half a century, Pyongyang has not launched an attack southward across the DMZ.[26]

The North Korean government has stated that it would use force only to defend itself and would not launch a first strike. The danger is that should Pyongyang feel that an attack on its territory is imminent, it may indeed launch such a strike to defend itself. Another important consideration is that North Korea views South Koreans as one people with the North.

The North Korean leadership appears to be fully aware of the South's economic potential. Although Pyongyang has made aggressive threats toward the United States, it has not directly threatened an attack on the South since the early 1990s, and it is unlikely to launch a military strike simply to reunify the country by force, given Seoul's current efforts to increase economic support to Pyongyang and the limited ability of the North Korean military to sustain an attack on the South. This, however, does not rule out the possibility of further military incidents involving North and South Korean forces.

So what, then, is the real threat from the North? The primary threat North Korea poses to the United States and regional security derives more from its illicit activities rather than the use of military force. While there remains a potential for the North to launch an attack through misunderstanding, fear that it is about to be attacked, or in an effort to prevent total collapse, the larger threats stem from the potential proliferation of North Korean missile or WMD technology to other countries or terrorist organizations. Additionally, North Korean efforts to gain hard currency through counterfeiting U.S. dollars or narcotics trafficking pose significant problems for the international community. Finally, North Korean human rights abuses and the ongoing refugee problem are having a significant impact on China and South Korea in particular.

CONCLUSION

Rather than advancing relations through a policy of engagement designed to increase U.S. ability to influence Pyongyang, the Bush administration chose a policy of nonengagement and isolation, which only served to limit the U.S. ability to both understand events inside of North Korea and to work productively with Pyongyang. It was not until the final 2 years of the administration that it appears a concerted effort was made to move toward a solution on the North Korean problem. However, as a result of the initial lack of progress, the Obama administration today finds itself faced with a North Korea that has a limited nuclear capability and continues to have little contact with the outside world. We have limited ability to gain an understanding of internal developments in the North and no clear policy for engaging Pyongyang or ensuring stability on the Korean Peninsula after Kim Jong Il dies.

ENDNOTES - CHAPTER 2

1. "The Plan Post Kim—No Plan," *Newsweek*, September 18, 2008, available from *www.newsweek.com/2008/09/12/the-plan-post-kim-no-plan.html*.

2. The Interagency Conflict Management Strategy Model was developed by Professor Robert Sharp at the National Defense University as a framework to provide a logical structured approach for thoroughly analyzing any international situation in a balanced manner and developing a coherent strategy—emphasizing ends, ways, and means to accomplish the desired outcome.

3. David Renne, "Rumsfeld Calls for Regime Change in North Korea," *The Daily Telegraph,* April 22, 2003, available from *www.commondreams.org/headlines03/0421-08.htm*.

4. *The National Security Strategy of the United States of America*, Washington, DC: The White House, 1999, pp. 1, 59-60.

5. *Ibid.*, pp. 14, 26-27.

6. *Ibid.*, pp. 3, 21, 40.

7. The 1994 Agreed Framework was negotiated during the Clinton administration. Among other things, it called for an end to North Korean nuclear development in return for U.S. economic and energy assistance. See Appendix 1.

8. *Background Note, North Korea*, Washington, DC: U.S. Department of State, Bureau of East Asian and Pacific Affairs, February 2009.

9. During former President Carter's visit in 1994, Kim Il Sung also agreed to allow the United States to search for missing soldiers from the Korean War. After extensive negotiations with North Korea, the first recovery missions were conducted in 1996. Approximately three-to-five recovery missions were conducted each year until the U.S. Government temporarily suspended operations in May 2005. Prior to that time, the remains of approximately 250 missing American soldiers had been recovered from sites north of Pyongyang and in the Chosin Reservoir area. These operations remain suspended since 2009.

10. Under Secretary of State for Political Affairs R. Nicholas Burns, Testimony before the House International Relations Committee on U.S. Policy Toward North Korea, November 16, 2006, available from *www.state.gov/p/us/rm/2006/76178.htm*.

11. Jonathan D. Pollack, "The United States, North Korea, and the End of the Agreed Framework," *Naval War College Review*, Summer 2003, pp. 14-16.

12. The Taepo Dong 2 has an estimated range of 3,500-7,000 km, enough to strike the western United States or Alaska. *Washington Post*, July 5, 2006, p. A10.

13. According to the Center for Non-Proliferation Studies, Monterey Institute of International Studies, the blast was the equivalent of "400-500 tons of TNT, with an upper bound of 800 tons." See "North Korea Conducts Nuclear Test," Monterey, CA: Center for Non-Proliferation Studies, 2006, available from *www. cns.miis.edu/pubs/week/pdf/061010_dprktest.pdf*.

14. Bradley K. Martin, *Under the Loving Care of the Fatherly Leader: North Korea and the Kim Dynasty*, New York: St Martin's Press, 2004, pp. 398-399.

15. It is often difficult for Westerners to truly understand the "god-like" status of Kim Il Sung and Kim Jong Il in the minds of the North Korean people. Kim Il Sung made thousands of trips around his country, giving "on-the-spot guidance" at worksites ranging from farms, to construction, to factory processes. His visits to these locations are marked by plaques, markers, and even glass cases. If he entered a room, a plaque is placed over the door, and the location is considered to be a sacred spot. Additionally, the birthplaces of Kim Il Sung, his parents, and his son, Kim Jong Il, are now shrines to which thousands of North Koreans visit each year. See Helen-Louise Hunter, *Kim Il-Song's North Korea*, Westport, CT: Praeger, 1999, pp. 14-16.

16. *Ibid.*, p. 399.

17. Scott Snyder, *Negotiating on the Edge: North Korean Negotiating Behavior*, Washington, DC: United States Institute of Peace Press, 1999, p. 39.

18. "Army First" emerged as a slogan in 1997. Under this policy, the Dear Leader instructed the people of North Korea "to concentrate greater efforts on military activities and strengthen national defense capabilities in every way–no matter how difficult the economic situation and no matter how great the financial burden." It essentially calls for giving the military priority over everything. William C. Triplett, *Rogue State: How a Nuclear North Korea Threatens America*, Washington, DC: Regnery Pub, 2004, p. 138.

19. *North Korea Can the Iron Fist Accept the Invisible Hand?* Seoul, South Korea: International Crisis Group, 2005, pp. 4-5.

20. *Washington Post*, March 9, 2009, p. A11.

21. Andrew Scobell, *Kim Jong Il and North Korea: The Leader and the System*, Carlisle, PA: Strategic Studies Institute, U.S. Army War College, 2006, p. 9.

22. Edward A. Olsen, "North Korea's Nuclear Acknowledgement: Motivation and Risks," *Strategic Insights*, Monterey, CA: Naval Post Graduate School, October 24, 2002, available from *www.ccc.nps.navy.mil/rsepResources/si/nov02/eastAsia.pdf*.

23. Richard Gunde, "North Korea a Greater Danger Than Iraq," Los Angeles, CA: University of California at Los Angeles International Institute, November 1, 2002, available from *www. international.ucla.edu/print.asp?parentid=2470*.

24. Scott Snyder, *Negotiating on the Edge: North Korean Negotiating Behavior*, Washington, DC: United States Institute of Peace Press, 1999, p. 145.

25. Christiana Amanpour, "Why Did North Korea Launch the Rocket?" *CNN*, April 6, 2009, available from *edition.cnn. com/2009/WORLD/asiapcf/04/06/amanpour.north.korea.rocket/index. html#cnnSTCText* .

26. Scobell, pp. 8-9.

CHAPTER 3

THE REGIONAL INTERESTS AND CULTURAL VIEWS

> South-North relations should be resolved smoothly with a more flexible and mature attitude. Last year marked the 60th anniversary of national division. It is about time the South and North overcame confrontation and conflict and opened a new age of cooperative coexistence and co-prosperity. I hope that North Korea will be able to read the change of the times and forge ahead with us for a bright future.
>
> South Korean President Lee Myung-bak
> January 2, 2009[1]

INTRODUCTION

In looking at the Korean Peninsula through the framework of the Interagency Conflict Management Strategy Model, we must consider the national interests and views of the United States, both North and South Korea, and the three key regional powers in northeast Asia: China, Russia, and Japan. Each country has specific national interests and concerns that will affect U.S. strategy and planning.

This chapter will first address U.S. national interests and perspectives on the Korean Peninsula. It will then look at the strategic interests of the key U.S. regional partners: China, Japan, Russia, and South Korea. Finally, it will address North Korea and its goals, its interests and the cultural influences on Pyongyang.

UNITED STATES AND REGIONAL INTERESTS

The United States.

The guiding principle for the United States in dealing with North Korea is to maintain a stable Korean Peninsula where people live in peace without the threat of war. In order to accomplish this goal, the specific U.S. national interests in relation to North Korea have included:

1. Eliminating all North Korean development and proliferation of weapons of mass destruction (WMD);

2. Reducing the threat of war on the Korean Peninsula;

3. Curtailing various illegal North Korean activities such as counterfeiting of currency and international weapons sales; and,

4. Weakening the regime or promoting regime change.

Much of the challenge faced by the United States in dealing with North Korea is the result of U.S. policymakers having limited knowledge and experience with North Korea and its people. There is little opportunity for travel to North Korea by Americans, no diplomatic relations or trade between the United States and North Korea, and no regular ongoing official U.S. contact. As a result of this lack of direct knowledge, it is very easy for U.S. policymakers to superimpose their own concept of the world on North Korea. Three examples of this come to mind. First, the widely held U.S. presumption that Kim Jong Il is an irrational and perhaps unstable leader. This notion appears to be anything but true.[2]

Second, the notion that North Koreans fear the Pyongyang regime and are waiting for any opportunity to overthrow it. Clearly, this concept shows a lack of understanding of the "god-like" status of both Kim Il Sung and Kim Jong Il, as discussed in Chapter 2. This notion also shows an incomplete understanding of the personal dynamics within North Korea, where the people are heavily influenced by the Confucian tradition of authority. Any indication of negative opinion toward the regime could lead to immediate negative consequences for both the individual involved and their family. This environment leaves little opportunity for any movement against the regime to develop. Moreover, there is no known indication of any organized internal threat to the Pyongyang regime.

Third, there is the often-stated idea that regime change is needed because North Koreans have a desire for democracy. This overlooks the fact that North Koreans have no real concept of democracy. The North Koreans have never experienced life in a democracy.

REGIONAL STRATEGIC CONCERNS

China.

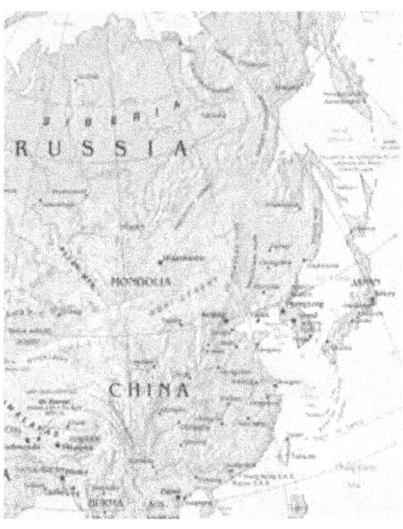

Map 3-1. Regional Map of China.[3]

China has a unique relationship with North Korea. As Pyongyang's only remaining Cold War ally, China has the closest relationship with North Korea of any of the countries in the region. This relationship goes back to the common bond they shared in fighting Japanese imperialism during World War II and Beijing's support of North Korea's fight against the United States in the Korean War. Of all nations in the region, China seems to be able to exert the most influence on North Korea. China's guiding principle regarding North Korea has been the maintenance of regional stability.

China has repeatedly stated three long-held principles that guide its policy toward the Korean Peninsula:[3]

1. The Korean Peninsula should be free of nuclear weapons;

2. Regional peace and stability must be maintained; and

3. The situation should be resolved through dialogue and negotiation.

From the perspective of the Chinese leadership, the most critical priorities for their country's policy toward North Korea are to:

1. Avoid the economic costs of an explosion on the Korean Peninsula;

2. Prevent the United States from dominating a unified Korea;

3. Secure the stability of its three economically weak northeastern provinces;[4]

4. Reduce the financial burden of their bilateral relationship with North Korea;

5. Be seen in a positive light for playing a major role in the denuclearization of the peninsula;

6. Use the situation in North Korea to leverage the United States on the issue of Taiwan; and,

7. Avoid North Korean situations that may provoke Japan to seek to be a nuclear power.[5]

China, along with the other countries in the region, is also acutely aware that a major event in Pyongyang could lead to a significant refugee crisis that affects the entire region.[6] Thus far, Beijing has been reluctant to discuss openly or participate in any potential planning for a possible collapse of the North Korean regime. Beijing may be concerned about alienating Pyongyang. Beijing's attitude may also be partly due to its long-standing policy of noninterference in the internal affairs of other countries. While Beijing, on occasion, has shown a degree of frustration with recent actions by Pyongyang, it continues to support the regime. In fact, China continues to be Pyongyang's major trading partner, accounting for more than 40 percent of North Korea's trade.[7]

Finally, China's conflicting regional, domestic, and international priorities make it unlikely that Beijing could be relied upon to force North Korea into any negotiations. It is also possible that Beijing may prefer to maintain a divided Korean Peninsula out of fear that a unified Korea may lead to greater instability in the region. Strategically, North Korea is currently a buffer between China and the democratic influence of Japan and South Korea. A collapse of the communist regime in Pyongyang could have a destabilizing effect on the northeastern Chinese regions. Also, the reunification of Korea would require a large investment by South Korea. This scenario is likely to reduce resources available for continued South Korean investment in China. China currently is the only country able to exert any influence on the Pyongyang regime. A unified Korea, aligned with the United States, would almost completely reduce any significant influence China might have over the Korean government.

Japan.

Events on the Korean Peninsula will have a major impact on Japanese security and prosperity going forward. As Tokyo is within range of North Korean missiles, Japan is deeply concerned about the potential for conflict on the Korean Peninsula. Economically, Japan could potentially benefit from trade relations with the North and access to raw materials. However, Tokyo has had a very difficult history with the region. There is a deep historical mistrust between Japan and Korea. The North Koreans have a long painful memory of their nearly half-century of life under Japanese imperial rule between 1905 and 1945. In many ways, the North Koreans dislike and fear the Japanese even more than they do the Americans.[8]

Japan's guiding principle and ideal is a unified Korea aligned with the United States rather than China, one that shares the political values of democracy, rule of law and a free market economy. Because of the historical mistrust between Korea and Japan, a key policy consideration from the Japanese perspective is an understanding that a unified Korea not aligned with the United States might be inclined to expand its military capabilities and eventually pose a threat to the Japanese territory and security.

Russia.

Russia is also concerned about regional stability. However, Moscow is also looking for an opportunity to reverse its loss of influence in the region since the fall of Communism. Economically, Moscow can gain significantly from access to warm water ports and the increased demand for Russian goods and energy resources that development in North Korea would bring.

The worst-case scenario for Russia would be a nationalist unified Korea closely aligned with China. Such a scenario would significantly limit Russia's influence and hinder its ability to develop oil and gas pipelines throughout the region. As a result, Russia is likely to support a unified Korea aligned toward the United States, along with a denuclearization of the peninsula.

South Korea.

The Seoul government is probably in the most complicated situation of all the countries in the region. While South Korea supports unification, the situation in the North potentially presents significant opportunities and tremendous burdens. The guiding principle for the Seoul government is the desire for regional stability and security. One key concern is the potential for conflict with the North. Seoul also worries that a hard collapse of North Korea would lead to an internal crisis. In addition, any drastic change in the North could ignite a massive refugee flow south. Finally, Seoul faces the looming challenge of providing sufficient economic and security aid to stabilize one of the most economically backward and politically isolated countries in the world. There is a very real possibility that Seoul could be quickly overwhelmed by any of these situations.[9]

Over the last 20 years, South Korean policy toward North Korea has varied considerably. Each South Korean government has had its own approach.

1. **Early 1990s — Kim Young Sam's —** *"Soft Landing Policy."* This policy emphasized providing assistance to North Korea in anticipation of an eventual collapse of the country following Kim Il Sung's death in 1994. This very public anticipation of North Korea's collapse prevented any real movement forward in inter-Korean relations.

2. **1998-2002 — Kim Dae Jung's** *"Sunshine Policy."* This policy marked a radical shift in South Korean strategy toward the North. It effectively separated economic issues from political issues. This policy, among other things, brought about a wide range of inter-Korean economic and cultural exchanges. However, it also saw little forward movement in inter-Korean relations because it did not address security confidence-building measures, and most of the exchanges were one way, from South to North.

3. **2002-07 — Roh Moo-Hyun's** *"Peace and Prosperity Policy."* This policy, built on previous efforts to promote inter-Korean reconciliation, was an effort to overhaul the "Sunshine Policy." However, it also failed because of the deepening domestic political divisions in South Korea over North Korean policy and concerns for the meager returns that had been achieved.

4. **2009 to the present — Lee Myung-Bak's** *"Denuclearization First Policy."* The first 18 months of the Lee Myung-Bak administration saw a progressive worsening of inter-Korean relations. In 2009, he proposed a policy that emphasized "one-step denuclearization" in return for massive incentives. These incentives included security guarantees and foreign assistance.

Seoul is very much aware of the economic investment potential in North Korea. Much of the South Korean efforts have focused on preparing to capitalize on this potential for economic opportunity in North Korea. The South Korean government has also used its economic leverage and family reunions to open channels of communication with the North Koreans.[10]

North Korea.

North Korea's primary goal and guiding principle has always been the preservation of the regime. It also wants to obtain sufficient economic and energy assistance to avoid starvation and other health problems. In addition to being recognized as a nuclear power, North Korea has consistently stated that it would like to see a negotiated solution to the nuclear issue, based on four conditions:[11]

1. U.S. recognition of North Korean sovereignty and noninterference in its internal affairs;

2. A nonaggression agreement with the United States;

3. Removal from the U.S. list of states sponsoring international terrorism;[12] and,

4. Noninterference by the United States in North Korea's economic development.

Additionally, North Korea has stated its desire for continued U.S. support of Korean unification, although not necessarily in the same form that South Korea envisions. Although there are similarities between the concepts of North and South Korea, there are also significant differences. North Korea has generally mentioned unification with a federation-type structure having a rotating leader. Under this concept, both North and South Korea would maintain their own government and economic structures.[13] Kim Il Sung provided the details for this concept for unification in his Report to the Sixth Congress of the Worker's Party of Korea on the Work of the Central Committee on October 10, 1980.[14] The North's federation is composed of one nation, one state, two governments, and two systems, whereas the South's confederation is composed of one nation, two states, two governments, and two systems. Essentially, both unification concepts comprise two regional governments with different political and economic systems.[15]

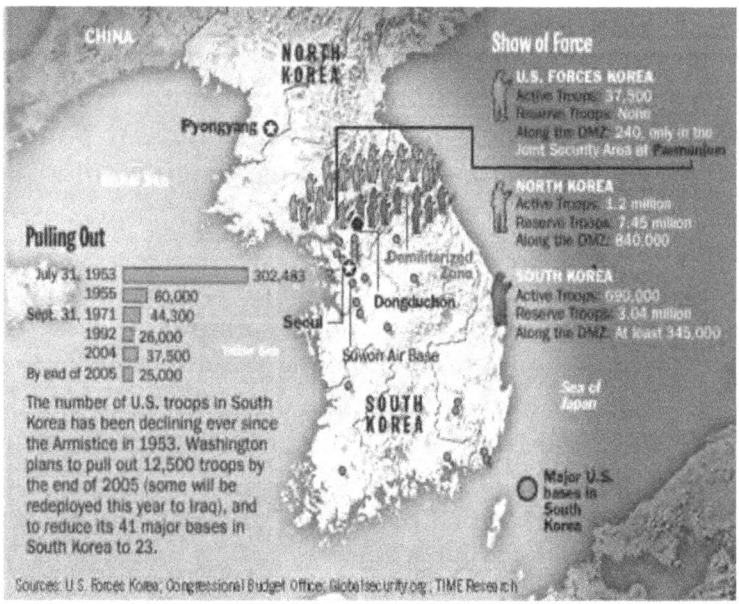

Note: Map 3-2 illustrates the U.S., North Korean, and South Korean forces on the Korean Peninsula. It is intended to show a comparison of the forces facing each other. This map also illustrates the pattern of reduction in U.S. forces on the Korean Peninsula since the end of the Korean War. A further, more detailed comparison of the military forces of North and South Korea can be found in Appendix 2.

Map 3-2. Comparison of North and South Korean Military Forces.

THE NORTH KOREAN CULTURAL ASPECT

In order to understand North Korean society, it is also important to understand the role that Confucian values have had on the society. According to Selig Harrison, Director of the Century Foundation's Project on the United States and the Future of Korea, "The ideal leader in Confucian ethos rules through the moral power of his exemplary behavior and the wisdom of his teachings, not through brutal coercion. Wisdom is handed down from the leader to the people, who learn what is 'correct' through the rote mastery of the truth."[16] Kim Il Sung, and later Kim Jong Il, were both able to successfully build on these Confucian ideals and virtues. Through the Confucian ideals, there was a built-in readiness within the Korean society for voluntary acceptance of strong authoritarian rule.

Another writer, Suk Hi Kim, editor of the *North Korean Review*, described the impact of Confucian traditions on North Korean society in this way:

> Despite a half century of Marxism, North Korea still consciously appropriates the powerful Confucian traditions of political centralization and obedience to authority that date back more than 6 centuries. The Confucian philosophy teaches that each person has his place in a hierarchical social order and that the preservation of harmony within the social order is of paramount importance. . . . (Both) Kim Il Sung and Kim Jong Il have consciously attempted to wrap themselves in the mantle of Confucian virtues. Thus, North Korea's tightly controlled system has lasted longer than any other 20th Century dictatorhip.[17]

Figure 3-1. North Korean Propaganda Image of Kim Jong Il Briefing Senior North Korean Military Leaders While Kim Il Sung Looks On. (Author's Collection.)

Influence of *Juche* on North Korean Society.

It is difficult to overestimate the role that the principle of *Juche*, or self-reliance, has played on the attitudes of North Koreans toward their country and leaders. The concept of *Juche* was first introduced by Sin Chae Ho, a Korean nationalist, in the early-20th century. Kim Il Sung ultimately made the concept a nationalist ideology, which eventually became the basis for the existence of North Korea. It was later transformed into a cult ideology by Kim Jong Il. *Juche* is constantly repeated in schools and the media and has come to be a powerful influence on North Koreans, emphasizing national self-reliance, independence, and the worship of the supreme leader. According to Suk Hi Kim, in his recent book, *North Korea at a Crossroads,*

> As *Juche* developed, the principle addressed several major issues. First, it served to maintain North Korea's independence. . . . Second, it also modeled North Kore-

ans into ever-loyal disciples of the leader. . . . Third, it glorified the solidarity of the people as a modern Confucian family around the party and its leader. Fourth, it defended the North Korean brand of socialism in the face of ever declining living standards. . . . Finally, . . . it gave the people a reason to live, even die for the regime. It seems that most people support the idea of *Juche* as a principle of national sovereignty, pride, and self-sufficiency.[18]

Potential for Open Rebellion to Develop in North Korea.

There must be a shared grievance needing correction by a changing society for change to occur. In fact, because of their extreme isolation from the outside world and the political repression that North Koreans have faced, most North Koreans do not even realize that they have any grievances (other than those against the United States and Japan). At least, it does not appear that they have any open grievances against the North Korean government. There has been little opportunity for any social movement to develop within North Korea. However, this could change with a precipitating event, such as the death of Kim Jong Il or an increased openness in North Korea.

Openness and democracy are double-edged swords with North Korea. As North Korea becomes more open to the outside world, restrictions on the population may gradually lift, and as more North Koreans begin to see and understand what the outside world is really like, grievances are likely to develop among the population. This will be particularly true as the North Koreans feel they have more freedom to express themselves without retribution. How the government handles these grievances is likely to determine whether or not the people will feel their grievances are being met. If the people feel grievances are not being met, they will move through this initial stage and begin violent actions toward the government.

CONCLUSION

The overall strategic concerns of China, Japan, Russia, and South Korea are focused around four key regional security issues:

1. Preventing the spread of nuclear weapons on the Korean Peninsula;

2. The potential for massive refugee flow were North Korea to collapse;

3. The potential for economic opportunity inside North Korea; and,

4. The potential security implications of a reunified Korea.

Each of these issues could cause potential problems throughout the region. China, in particular, is acutely aware of the potential refugee problems and the impact that these problems might have on Chinese territory. South Korea, on the other hand, is significantly focused on the potential for economic opportunity in North Korea. Japan is acutely focused on security concerns evolving from a spread of nuclear weapons to the Korean Peninsula. North Korea remains focused on preservation of the regime.

ENDNOTES - CHAPTER 3

1. *Korea Times*, January 2, 2009, available from *www.korea-times.co.kr/www/news/nation/2009/01/116_37212.html*.

2. According to Oh and Hassig, "Pyongyang's leaders' reasoning is likely constrained or limited by the view from where

they sit gazing out on the world. North Korea's rulers are influenced by history, ideology, and notions of nationalism that produce what social scientists term a 'bounded rationality'." Kong Dan Oh and Ralph Hassig, *North Korea Through the Looking Glass*, Washington, DC: The Brookings Institution Press, 2000, p. 192.

3. *CIA World Factbook 2009*, New York: Skyhorse Publishing, Inc., 2008.

4. *China and North Korea: Comrades Forever?* International Crisis Group (ICG) Asia Report, No. 112, Seoul, South Korea: International Crisis Group, 2006, p. 5.

5. China has an approximately 1,400 km land border with North Korea affecting these northeastern provinces.

6. ICG, p. i.

7. A recent Council on Foreign Relations study projected that a hard crash in North Korea could lead to as many as one million refugees attempting to cross its borders. The projection estimated as many as 500,000 North Korean refugees would cross into China, 200,000 into Russia or Japan, and 300,000 into South Korea. Paul B. Stares and Joel S. Wit, *Preparing for Sudden Change in North Korea*, New York: Council on Foreign Relations, 2009, p. 21.

8. This is double the North Korean trade with South Korea and six times the trade with Japan in 2005. *Ibid.*, p. 3.

9. Although there are no accurate figures for North Korea, a recent study indicated that in 2002, 66 percent of the members of the South Korean National Assembly selected Japan as the biggest potential threat to East Asia. The South Korean public listed Japan as the second biggest threat (21 percent) after North Korea (54 percent). It ranked China only as a distant third (8 percent). Hideki Yamaji, *Policy Recommendations for Japan Unification of the Korean Peninsula*, Washington, DC: The Brookings Institution Center for Northeast Asian Policy Studies, 2004, p. 13.

10. While the closed North Korean society makes it difficult to get an accurate estimate of the total cost of unification, a recent report by the South Korean National Assembly's Special Com-

mittee on Budget and Accounts estimated that the cost to South Korea would be between $850 billion and $1.3 trillion. Jong Sung-ki, "Unification of Koreas to Cost $1.3 Trillion," *Korea Times,* October 28, 2007, available from *www.koreatimes.co.kr/www/news/nation/2007/10/113_12637.html* .

11. According to a recent Congressional Research Service Report,

> [Seoul's] strategy has been to use its economic leverage and family reunions (families separated by the division of the Korean Peninsula) to open channels with the North Korean people. . . . Seoul also recognizes that its economic ties are gradually shifting from reliance on the American market to greater integration with China, Japan, and other countries of Asia. Its labor costs are rising, and many of its companies are remaining competitive only by manufacturing in China and other low-wage markets. For them, the prospect of abundant cheap labor just a short distance to the north is appealing and perhaps an alternative to cheap labor in China.

Dick Nanto, Dick Kazuyuki, and Emma Chanlett-Avery, *The North Korean Economy Leverage and Policy Analysis*, CRS report for Congress, RL32493, Washington, DC: Congressional Research Service, Library of Congress, 2008, p. 41.

12. *North Korea: A Phased Negotiation Strategy*, ICG Asia Report, No. 61, Washington, DC: ICG, 2003, p. 23.

13. North Korea was removed from the list of states supporting terrorism by President Bush in 2008.

14. Young W. Kihl and Hong Nack Kim, *North Korea: The Politics of Regime Survival*, Armonk, NY: M. E. Sharpe, 2006, pp. 232-236.

15. See *Song Gun Politics Study Group* Website, available from *www.songunpoliticsstudygroup.org/Oct102008/W-801010.HTM.*

16. Young-Sun H, *Conflicting Visions for Korean Reunification*, Fellows paper—Weatherhead Center for International Affairs, Cambridge, MA: Harvard University, 2001, p. 20.

17. Selig S. Harrison, *Korean Endgame: A Strategy for Reunification and U.S. Disengagement*, Princeton, NJ: Princeton University Press, 2002, p. 23.

18. Suk H. Kim, *North Korea at a Crossroads*, Jefferson, NC: Mc-Farland & Co, 2003, p. 54.

19. *Ibid.*, pp. 55-56.

CHAPTER 4

DEVELOPING A STRATEGY

Dealing with North Korea is perhaps one of the most difficult security challenges in global politics today. Totalitarian and reclusive, ideologically isolated and economically ruined, it is the inherent 'other' in a globalized and neoliberal world order.

Roland Bleiker
Author of "Divided North Korea:
Toward a Culture of Reconciliation[1]

INTRODUCTION

Clearly, there are significant differences between North and South Korea that were not present between East and West Germany in 1990. Among these differences is the fact that, unlike the North Koreans, the East Germans were not completely isolated from the outside world. They had an awareness of the world around them, understood democracy, and wanted unification to occur. In the case of North Korea, the population as a whole knows little about South Korea and even less about the outside world. Although the Pyongyang leadership talks about potential unification in positive terms, it is not clear what its reaction would be to unification if the South Korean government were in a leadership role.

Two other very important differences between North Korea and East Germany are: first, the lack of any real middle class in North Korea. In the case of East Germany, it was the middle class frustration with the pace of reform that led to the fall of the Berlin Wall and collapse of the communist system. Second, unlike East Germany, North Korea possesses a nuclear capability. This North Korean nuclear capability significantly changes the political and security dynamics of the Korean Peninsula and may require different actions to ensure safety and security.

Despite these differences, there are many areas where we can learn from the German example. In the case of the German Reunification, the United States and regional powers played a major role in setting the conditions for a peaceful reunification. In the Korean case, first and foremost, the Obama administration must determine the U.S. strategy for dealing with North Korea and its potential collapse. The administration must determine how the U.S. Government sees the Korean Peninsula evolving over the coming decade if we want to have any impact on shaping the future events in the region. U.S. strategy must also consider the broader strategic environment in the region, particularly China's role as a key player in northeast Asia and a potential supporter or detractor of U.S. strategy. Furthermore, strategy should center on South Korea as being the legitimate Korean government and provide support for the peaceful unification of North and South Korea. The key U.S. goal should be peaceful reunification with stability, both on the Korean Peninsula and in the region.

Much as was done in the case of the German Reunification, the Obama administration will need to embark on a period of public diplomacy to sell the strategy, both to the American public and U.S. regional partners. Policymakers must understand that we will not be able to accomplish any of the U.S. strategic goals toward the Korean Peninsula without the active support of China and Russia. We can help ease Chinese security fears and gain China's cooperation by working with Beijing to address and reduce these concerns. One possible approach would be to indicate that no U.S. troops would enter North Korea unless the security and stability of the Korean Peninsula required U.S. troops. In the case of Russia, we can help gain its support by addressing its desire to have renewed influence in the region, and by ensuring Russian concerns are taken into account in any discussions.

In the case of North Korea, we must keep in mind that, despite all the hardships and difficulties it has suffered, its population is a proud people. They have been taught since they were very young that they have accomplished much, and they believe it. We must treat North Korea as we would any other country. Therefore, any U.S. policy should emphasize engagement with North Korea first and foremost. This engagement should include discussions, negotiations, cultural exchanges, and even diplomatic relations. Only by engaging North Korea will we begin to understand each other, and only then will we have some level of positive influence on them.[2] We must work within the context of maintaining flexibility so that neither side loses "face" in discussions. We must also realize that we cannot expect the North to take positive actions without giving them something in return.

As Ambassador Charles Pritchard, former U.S. Special Envoy for Negotiations with the Democratic People's Republic of Korea (DPRK) during the Clinton administration, points out in his recent book:

> To enter negotiations toward achieving normalization (with North Korea) requires Washington to make a strategic decision—which it has not made—to accept North Korea's system of government and leadership much as it has the Chinese, Vietnamese, Russian. . . . Normalization of relations . . . does require the United

States to refrain from efforts to change the regime, but it does not mean . . . forgo(ing) serious engagement on humanitarian issues and monetary security.[3]

Although it will be difficult, a policy of actively engaging North Korea will eventually provide the United States with a forum to exert a limited degree of influence on the Pyongyang leadership. It will also give us a better understanding of what is actually happening inside North Korea. Ultimately, we must keep in mind that, as in the case of Eastern Europe, events on the ground are likely to outpace any planning we do. It will be extremely critical that we have both an awareness of events as they are occurring and the flexibility of action to ensure appropriate measured responses.

DEVELOPING A U.S. STRATEGY

In developing U.S. strategy for the Korean Peninsula, it is essential that we work closely with our regional partners — China, Russia, South Korea, and Japan — to develop a common framework for discussion and planning on the future of the peninsula. Ultimately, any U.S. strategy toward North Korea must include economic, diplomatic, and military elements. U.S. strategy should be aimed at accomplishing the transformation of North Korea in three areas:

1. The North Korean perceived threat from the United States and the West.

2. The nature of the North Korean government and the ruling regime.

3. The North Korean economic system.

U.S. policy towards North Korea must also:

1. Recognize that threats of the use of force and no contact are counterproductive in dealing with North Korea. One of the most productive things we could do is reach agreement on ending the armistice from the Korean War and giving a formal security guarantee to North Korea tied to nonproliferation of weapons of mass destruction (WMD).

2. Restart the Joint U.S.-North Korean Missing In Action (MIA) discussions and searches inside North Korea. This will give the United States an opportunity for formal direct government engagement and contact with the North Korean military leadership.

3. Look at providing alternative energy sources for North Korea tied to developing a verifiable limit to North Korea's nuclear development in return.

4. Move gradually toward establishing diplomatic relations with North Korea. Start with a U.S. Interests section or a Consulate in Pyongyang. Initiate formal high-level contacts outside the Six-Party Talks and gradually move toward establishing full diplomatic relations.

These actions would put us in a position to influence events on the Korean Peninsula and encourage movement toward a soft collapse. The most difficult burden, however, will be placed on South Korea, and we must be prepared to support Seoul politically, financially, and logistically.

The United States must begin working with Seoul to plan actions that address the security, governance and participation, economic stabilization and infrastructure, humanitarian assistance and social well-being, and justice and reconciliation issues that it will face in unifying with North Korea. Much will depend on the political leadership of both U.S. regional partners and the North. If we are able to successfully influence regional partners to begin moving forward on unification discussions, then both North and South Korea should begin serious planning efforts to bring the two countries together. The most critical consideration will be maintaining stability in the North.

The Obama administration has several specific policy options to consider in determining its strategy toward North Korea. Each option carries a degree of risk.

1. Continue the current U.S. policy toward North Korea. This includes the use of economic sanctions, efforts to eliminate North Korea's nuclear capability, and emphasis on the Six-Party Talks.

2. Intensify sanctions aimed at forcing North Korean compliance.

3. Move to normalize relations with North Korea, sign a formal peace treaty ending the Korean War, begin bilateral discussions, and accept that North Korea will maintain its limited nuclear capability.

ENDNOTES - CHAPTER 4

1. Roland Bleiker, *Divided Korea: Towards Cultural Reconciliation*, Minneapolis, MN: University of Minnesota Press, 2005, p. ix.

2. North Korea has consistently stated that it is seeking U.S. recognition, aid, and an easing of trade sanctions. Antoaneta Bezlova, "China: Calm Over Planned North Korean Missile Launch," *Inter Press Service News Agency,* April 8, 2009, available from *www. ipsnews.net/print.asp?idnews=46209.*

3. Charles L. Pritchard, *Failed Diplomacy: The Tragic Story of How North Korea Got the Bomb*, Washington, DC: The Brookings Institution Press, 2007, p. 143.

CHAPTER 5

CONCLUSION

> Unification of the two Koreas is a long cherished de-
> sire of the 70 million Korean people. Inter-Korean re-
> lations must become more productive than they are
> now. Our attitude will be pragmatic, not ideological.
> The core task is to help all Koreans live happily and to
> prepare the foundation for unification.
>
> South Korean President Lee Myung-bak
> February 25, 2008[1]

Despite some pronounced differences between
East Germany and North Korea, there are lessons we
can use in planning for a Korean unification. The most
important and critical lesson may be that of the role
of the United States and its allies. The U.S. Government had a strategy for handling German unification
and was able to sell it to the key European nations
and the Soviet Union. The United States does not currently have a strategy or a plan for shaping a Korean
unification and the Korean Peninsula once Kim Jong
Il dies. As a result, the United States has little influence on North Korea and is put in a position of react-
ing to events rather than shaping them. The Obama
administration has an opportunity to develop such a
plan and begin moving in a direction that will enable
United States to influence events in North Korea in the
coming years.

Internally, the rigid isolation and political indoctri-
nation of the North Korean people make it very unlikely that the German example of a quick takeover would
be successful. In all likelihood, such a takeover would
be likely to meet significant resistance in the North.

The ideal approach to Korean unification may be a slower path where the two countries unify under an overarching political structure, but initially maintain their own separate political and military structures. Although slower, such a course may provide for more stability. Economic and social changes could then be addressed gradually, while maintaining political and security stability. As changes took effect, the North could then gradually be moved closer to the South Korean model. Over a period of time, as economic and social conditions began to improve, the South Korean political system could take root in the North, and the North Korean political and military leadership could gradually be retired.

The Obama administration has the opportunity to move toward peace on the Korean Peninsula. To do this, however, it will have to deal with North Korea on the same level as it deals with any other country. First and foremost, U.S. policy must emphasize engagement with Pyongyang. This engagement should include discussions, negotiations, cultural exchanges, and even diplomatic relations. As stated previously, we must engage North Korea on multiple levels if our two nations are to begin to develop a mutual understanding. This understanding is essential if the United States is ever to have any positive influence on Pyongyang. We must also endeavor to remain flexible to ensure that neither side loses "face" in discussions and understand that we cannot expect North Korea to undertake positive actions without giving them something they want in return.

According to Roland Bleiker, a former Swiss diplomat in North Korea, "Dialogue is undoubtedly one of the most needed and, until recently, least practiced features that could generate a more peaceful political environment in Korea. Dialogue is essential for diffusing tension and preventing the risk of violence."[2] While this may seem counterintuitive to some, we only need look at the U.S. inability to influence or fully understand North Korea. It is difficult for any nation to influence or have an impact on another if it refuses to engage.

We must also recognize that threats of the use of force along with no contact are counterproductive in dealing with North Korea. An agreement on ending the armistice from the Korean War and giving a formal security guarantee to North Korea is probably one of the most productive things we can do. Ultimately, U.S. policy should move gradually toward establishment of diplomatic relations with North Korea. While North Korea's primary goal is and has been preservation of the regime, the United States can work within that goal by providing economic and medical assistance. As relations improve, we are likely to gradually develop a position of some influence over the regime, much as we have done in China and Vietnam.

North Korea's leadership has consistently stated that it would like to see a negotiated solution to the nuclear issue based on these four conditions:

1. U.S. recognition of North Korean sovereignty;

2. Noninterference in its internal affairs;

3. A nonaggression agreement with the United States; and,

4. Noninterference by the United States in North Korea's economic development.

By engaging with North Korea, we may eventually be in a position to influence the actions of the North Korean leadership.

This is not to suggest that any of this will be easy or happen quickly. North Korea is a difficult nation with which to negotiate and often reacts in a manner that outside observers see as counterproductive. It is also important to understand that a policy of engagement is really a double-edged sword for the North Korean leadership. North Korea's biggest weakness may, in fact, be opening up to the West. When this begins to happen, there is a significant potential for the regime to be weakened. Yet North Korea's current economic situation leaves its leadership few options. North Koreans seem to understand that they must work with the United States and other nations in order to get assistance. However, the more its people are able to see and have contact with Americans and others Westerners, the more they will start to see what they really do not have and cannot achieve under the current regime. When that happens, North Korea's challenge will be how to control the population's expectations and grievances so that they do not resort to violence.

The North Korean leadership has seen the examples of the Soviet Union and China and will surely approach any engagement effort by the United States with caution. In the end, however, we can only hope to get to a peaceful unification by developing a sound strategy and working with, rather than isolating North Korea.

ENDNOTES - CHAPTER 5

1. President Lee Myung-bak's Inaugural Address, February, 25, 2008, available from *www.docstoc.com/docs/44058469/President-Lee-Myung-baks-Inaugural-Address*.

2. Roland Bleiker, *Divided Korea: Toward a Culture of Reconciliation*, Minneapolis, MN: University of Minnesota Press, 2005, p. xli.

APPENDIX I

THE AGREED FRAMEWORK AND ITS IMPORTANCE

The "Agreed Framework," as it was known, was signed by the United States and North Korea on October 21, 1994. The key elements of this document included the following:[1]

1. Both sides will cooperate to replace North Korea's (DPRK) graphite-moderated reactors and related facilities with light-water reactors (LWR).

- The United States will organize an international consortium to build LWRs.
- The United States will supply 500,000 tons of heavy fuel oil annually to replace the energy of the closed graphite-moderated reactors until the LWRs are completed.
- As soon as the agreement goes into effect, the DPRK will freeze graphite moderated reactors. They will be dismantled when the LWRs are completed.
- The United States and the DPRK will cooperate to make sure that the spent fuel rods from the DPRK's graphite moderated reactors are properly stored during construction of the LWRs, and will dispose of them when the LWRs are completed without them being reprocessed in the DPRK.

2. The two sides will move toward full normalization of political and economic relations.

- Barriers to trade and investment will be removed.

- Each side will open a liaison office in the other's capital.
- As progress is made on other issues, the two countries will upgrade relations to the ambassadorial level.

3. Both sides will work together for peace and security on a nuclear-free Korean Peninsula.
- The United States will provide formal assurances to the DPRK against the threat or use of nuclear weapons by the United States.
- The DPRK will consistently make steps to implement the North-South Joint Declaration on the Denuclearization of the Korean Peninsula.
- The DPRK will engage in north-south dialogue.

4. Both sides will work together to strengthen the international nuclear nonproliferation regime.
- The DPRK will continue to remain in the Treaty on the Nonproliferation of Nuclear Weapons (NPT).
- Upon conclusion of the supply contract for the provision of the LWR, ad hoc and routine inspections will resume under the DPRK's agreement with the International Atomic Energy Agency (IAEA) with respect to facilities not subject to the freeze.
- When progress is sufficient in the LWR, the DPRK will come into full compliance with its safeguards agreement with the IAEA.

ENDNOTES - APPENDIX I

1. Agreed Framework between the United States of America and the Democratic People's Republic of Korea Geneva, Switzerland, October 21, 1994, available from *www.kedo.org/pdfs/Agreed-Framework.pdf*.

APPENDIX II

COMPARISON OF MILITARY CAPABILITIES
BETWEEN SOUTH AND NORTH KOREA

Classification				South Korea	North Korea
Troops (Peace time)		Total		More than 674,000	More than 1,170,000
		Army		541,000	1,000,000
		Navy		68,000	60,000
		Air Force		65,000	110,000
Principal Force Capability	Army	Units	Corps	12 (including Special Warfare Command)	19 (including the Artillery corps, Missile guidance bureau and light infantry instruction guidance bureau)
			Divisions	50	75
			Maneuver Brigade	19	69 (excluding 10 instruction guidance brigades)
		Equipment	Tanks	2,300	3,700
			Armored vehicles	2,500	2,100
			Field artillery	5,100	8,500
			MLRS	200	4,800
			Surface-to-surface guided weapons	20 (launchers)	80 (launchers)
	Navy	Surface ships	Warships	120	420
			Landing vessels	10	260
			Mine warfare ships	10	30
			Support vessels	20	30
		Submarines		10	60
	Air Force	Fighters		500	820
		Special aircraft		80 (including naval aircraft)	30
		Support aircraft		190	510
		Helicopters		680 (including all helicopters of the 3 services)	310
Reserve Forces (troops)				3,040,000	7,700,700 (including the instruction guidance units, Worker/Peasant red guard units and Red youth guard)
*	Naval troops of South Korea include 25,000 troops of ROK Marine Corps and Ground Forces units(Division/Brigade) and equipment include those of Marine Corps.				
**	The field artillery of the North does not include infantry regiment's 76.2mm guns.				
***	Owning to limitation as for the expression of qualitative assessment, the above table indicates only quantitative comparison at the level of opening to the public.				

Source: Republic of Korea, Ministry of Unification, available from www.unikorea.go.kr/eng/default.jsp?pgname=NORtables.

BIBLIOGRAPHY

An, Chung-yŏng, Nick Eberstadt, and Yŏng-sŏn Yi. *A New International Engagement Framework for North Korea? Contending Perspectives*, Washington, DC: Korea Economic Institute of America, 2004.

Bae, Jin-Young, "The Fiscal Burden of Korean Reunification and Its Impact on South Korea's Macroeconomic Stability," *Joint U.S.-Korea Academic Studies*, Vol. 6, 1996, pp. 185-202.

Bechtol, Bruce E, *Red Rogue: The Persistent Challenge of North Korea*, Washington, DC: Potomac Books, 2007.

Becker, Jasper, *Rogue Regime: Kim Jong Il and the Looming Threat of North Korea*. Oxford, UK: Oxford University Press, 2005.

Bleiker, Roland, *Divided Korea: Toward a Culture of Reconciliation*. Minneapolis, MN: University of Minnesota Press, 2005.

Breen, Michael, *The Koreans: Who They Are, What They Want, Where Their Future Lies*, New York: St. Martin's Press, 1999.

Carpenter, Ted Galen and Doug Bandow, *The Korean Conundrum: America's Troubled Relations with North and South Korea*, New York: Palgrave Macmillan, 2004.

Chong, Bong-uk, *North Korea, the Land That Never Changes: Before and After Kim Il-Sung*, Seoul, Republic of Korea: Naewoe Press, 1995.

Cucullu, Gordon, *Separated at Birth; How North Korea Became the Evil Twin*, Guilford, CT: Lyons Press, 2004.

Eberstadt, Nicholas, "The Persistence of North Korea: What Has Been Keeping Pyongyang Afloat?" *Policy Review*, October-November 2004.

Flassbeck, Heiner and Gustav Horn, *German Unification: An Example for Korea?* Brookfield, WI: Ashgate Publishing Company, 1996.

French, Paul, *North Korea: The Paranoid Peninsula – a Modern History*, London, UK: Zed Books, 2005.

Galgano, Francis Anthony and Eugene Joseph Palka, *North Korea*, Geographic Perspectives, Guilford, CT: McGraw-Hill/Dushkin, 2004.

Garner, Shelly Renae, *The "Two Plus Four" Talks and the Resolution of the External Aspects of German Unification*, Thesis (M.A.), Columbia, SC: University of South Carolina, 1992.

Goldstein, Frank L. and Frank E. Emmett, *A Psychological Perspective on the People within the Democratic People's Republic of Korea (DPRK)*, U.S. Strategic Command, April 18, 2004.

Gunde, Richard, *North Korea a Greater Danger than Iraq*, Los Angeles, CA: University of California at Los Angeles International Institute, November 1, 2002, available from *www.international. ucla.edu/print.asp?parentid=2470*.

Haggard, Stephan and Marcus Noland, *Famine in North Korea: Markets, Aid, and Reform*, New York: Columbia University Press, 2007.

Hart-Landsberg, Martin, *Korea: Division, Reunification, and U.S. Foreign Policy*, New York: Monthly Review Press, 1998.

Harrison, Selig S., *Korean Endgame: A Strategy for Reunification and U.S. Disengagement*, Princeton, NJ: Princeton University Press, 2002.

Hassig, Kongdan O., Joseph S. Bermudez, Jr., Kenneth E. Gause, Ralph C. Hassig, and Alexandre Y. Mansourov, *North Korean Policy Elites*, Ft. Belvoir, VA: Defense Technical Information Center, 2004, available from *handle.dtic.mil/100.2/ADA427588*.

Heilemann, Ullrich and Hermann Rappen, *The Seven Year Itch? German Unity from a Fiscal Viewpoint*, Washington, DC: American Institute for Contemporary German Studies, 1997.

Howard, P., "Why Not Invade North Korea? Threats, Language Games, and U.S. Foreign Policy," *International Studies Quarterly.* Vol. 48, No. 4, 2004, pp. 805-828.

Hunter, Helen-Louise, *Kim Il-Song's North Korea*, Westport, CT: Praeger, 1999.

International Crisis Group (ICG), *North Korea: A Phased Negotiation Strategy*, ICG Asia report, No. 61, Washington, DC: ICG, 2003.

_____, *China and North Korea: Comrades Forever?* ICG Asia Report, No. 112, Seoul, South Korea: ICG, 2006.

_____, *Japan and North Korea Bones of Contention*, Seoul, Korea: ICG, 2005, available from *bibpurl.oclc.org/web/10952*.

_____, *North Korea: Can the Iron Fist Accept the Invisible Hand?* Seoul, Korea: ICG, 2005, available from *bibpurl.oclc.org/web/9903*.

Ji, Young-Sun, *Conflicting Visions for Korean Re-unification*, Fellows paper — Weatherhead Center for International Affairs, Cambridge, MA: Harvard University, 2001.

Kaplan, Robert D., "When North Korea Falls," *The Atlantic Monthly*, Vol. 298, No. 3, October 2006, available from *www.theatlantic.com/doc/200610/kaplan-korea*.

Kihl, Young W. and Hong Nack Kim, *North Korea: The Politics of Regime Survival*, Armonk, NY: M. E. Sharpe, 2006.

Kim, Samuel S., *North Korean Foreign Relations in the Post-Cold War World*, Demystifying North Korea Series, Carlisle, PA: Strategic Studies Institute, U.S. Army War College, 2007, available from *www.strategicstudiesinstitute.army.mil/pdffiles/PUB772.pdf*.

Kim, Samuel S., ed., *The North Korean System in the Post-Cold War Era*, New York: Palgrave, 2001.

_____, *Inter-Korean Relations: Problems and Prospects*, New York: Palgrave Macmillan, 2004.

Kim, Suk H., *North Korea at a Crossroads,* Jefferson, NC: McFarland & Co, 2003.

Korea (South), *The Road to Korean Unification,* Seoul, Korea: Korean Ministry of Unification, 2008.

Lee, Hy-Sang, *North Korea: A Strange Socialist Fortress,* Westport, CT: Praeger, 2000.

Martin, Bradley K., *Under the Loving Care of the Fatherly Leader: North Korea and the Kim Dynasty,* New York: St Martin's Press, 2004.

Nanto, Dick Kazuyuki and Emma Chanlett-Avery, *The North Korean Economy Leverage and Policy Analysis,* CRS Report for Congress, RL32493, Washington, DC: Congressional Research Service, Library of Congress, 2008, available from *www.fas.org/sgp/crs/row/RL32493.pdf.*

Niksch, Larry A., *North Korea's Nuclear Weapons Development and Diplomacy,* CRS Report for Congress, RL33590, Washington, DC: Congressional Research Service, Library of Congress, 2008, available from *www.fas.org/sgp/crs/row/RL33590.pdf.*

Noland, Marcus, *The Economics of Korean Unification,* Washington, DC: Peterson Institute for International Economics, 2007.

Noland, Marcus, ed., *Economic Integration of the Korean Peninsula,* Policy Special Report 10, Washington, DC: Institute for International Economics, 1998.

Noland, Marcus, Sherman Robinson, and LiGang Liu, "The Costs and Benefits of Korean Unification," *Asian Survey,* Vol. XXXVIII, No. 8, August 1998, pp. 801-814.

Oh, Kong Dan, *Leadership Change in North Korean Politics: The Succession to Kim Il Sung,* Santa Monica, CA: Rand, 1988.

Oh, Kong Dan and Ralph Hassig, *North Korea through the Looking Glass,* Washington, DC: The Brookings Institution Press, 2000.

O'Hanlon, Michael O. and Mike Mochizuki, *Crisis on the Korean Peninsula: How to Deal with a Nuclear North Korea,* New York: McGraw Hill, 2003.

Olsen, Edward A., "North Korea's Nuclear Acknowledgement: Motivation and Risks," *Strategic Insights*, Monterey, CA: Naval Post Graduate School, October 24, 2002, available from *www.ccc.nps.navy.mil/rsepResources/si/nov02/eastAsia.pdf.*

Orr, Robert C., *Winning the Peace: An American Strategy for Post-Conflict Reconstruction*, Significant Issues Series, Vol. 26, No. 7, Washington, DC: Center for Strategic and International Studies (CSIS) Press, 2004.

Park, Kyung-Ae and Tal-chung Kim, *Korean Security Dynamics in Transition*, New York: Palgrave, 2001.

Pinkston, D. A. and P. C. Saunders, 2003, "Seeing North Korea Clearly," *Survival.* Vol. 45, pp. 79-102.

Pollack, Jonathan D., "The United States, North Korea, and the End of the Agreed Framework," *Naval War College Review*, Summer 2003, pp. 14-16.

Republic of Korea, Ministry of Unification, *The Road to Korean Reunification,* Seoul, Korea: Ministry of Unification, 2009.

Republic of Korea, *Ministry of Unification Website,* available from *www.unikorea.go.kr/eng/default.jsp?pgname=POLworkplan.*

Scobell, Andrew, *Kim Jong Il and North Korea: The Leader and the System,* Carlisle, PA: Strategic Studies Institute, U.S. Army War College, 2006.

_____, *Projecting Pyongyang*, Demystifying North Korea, Vol. 7, Carlisle, PA: Strategic Studies Institute, U.S. Army War College, 2008, available from *purl.access.gpo.gov/GPO/LPS92390.*

Scobell, Andrew and John M. Sanford, *North Korea's Military Threat: Pyongyang's Conventional Forces, Weapons of Mass Destruction, and Ballistic Missiles*, Demystifying North Korea Series, Carlisle, PA: Strategic Studies Institute, U.S. Army War College, 2007. Available from *www.strategicstudiesinstitute.army.mil/pdffiles/PUB 771.pdf.*

_____, *North Korea's Strategic Intentions*, Demystifying North Korea Series, Carlisle, PA: Strategic Studies Institute, U.S. Army War College, 2005, available from *purl.access.gpo.gov/GPO/LPS63250.*

Seliger, B., "Unified Germany's Security Policy: Some Lessons for Korea," *Korean Journal of Defense Analsis,* Vol. 15, No. 1, 2003, pp. 183-200.

Smith, Hazel, *Reconstituting Korean Security: A Policy Primer*, Tokyo, Japan: United Nations University Press, 2007.

_____, *Hungry for Peace: International Security, Humanitarian Assistance, and Social Change in North Korea*, Washington, DC: United States Institute of Peace, 2005.

Snyder, Scott, *Negotiating on the Edge: North Korean Negotiating Behavior,* Washington, DC: United States Institute of Peace Press, 1999.

Stares, Paul B. and Joel S. Wit, *Preparing for Sudden Change in North Korea*, New York: Council on Foreign Relations, 2009, available from *www.cfr.org/content/publications/attachments/North_Korea_CSR42.pdf.*

Stark, Rodney, *Sociology*, 4th Ed., Belmont, CA: Wadsworth Publishing Co, 1992.

Steinberg, Dana, "Newly Available Evidence Offers Insights Into North Korea's Thinking, Actions," Washington, DC: Woodrow Wilson International Center for Scholars, available from *www.wilsoncenter.org/index.cfm?topic_id=1409&fuseaction=topics.item&news_id=11681.*

Suh, Dae-Sook and Chae-Jin Lee, *North Korea After Kim Il Sung*, Boulder, CO: Lynne Rienner Publishers, 1998.

Triplett, William C., *Rogue State: How a Nuclear North Korea Threatens America*, Washington, DC: Regnery Pub, 2004.

United States, *Background Note, North Korea*, Washington, DC: U.S. Department of State, Bureau of East Asian and Pacific Affairs, February 2009, available from *purl.access.gpo.gov/GPO/LPS33761.*

_____,*The National Security Strategy of the United States of America*, Washington, DC: The White House, 2006, available from *purl.access.gpo.gov/GPO/LPS67777.*

_____,*The National Security Strategy of the United States of America*, Washington, DC: The White House, 2002.

_____, *The National Security Strategy of the United States of America*, Washington, DC: The White House, 1999.

_____, *CIA World Factbook 2009*, New York: Skyhorse Publishing Co., Inc, 2008.

Vaknin, Sam, "The Cost of Unification - German Lessons for Korea," *Global Politician*, 2005, available from *www.globalpolitician. com/2483-korea.*

Weathersby, Kathryn, "The Enigma of the North Korean Regime: Back to the Future?" *Ilmin International Relations Review*, Vol. 10, No. 1, Spring 2005, pp. 235-266.

Wolf, Charles and Norman D. Levin, *Modernizing the North Korean System: Objectives, Method, and Application*, Santa Monica, CA: RAND Corporation, 2008.

Wolf, Charles and Kamil Akramov, *North Korean Paradoxes: Circumstances, Costs, and Consequences of Korean Unification*, Santa Monica, CA: RAND Corporation, 2005.

Yamaji, Hideki, *Policy Recommendations for Japan Unification of the Korean Peninsula*, CNAPS working paper series, 2004, Washington, DC: The Brookings Institution Center for Northeast Asian Policy Studies, 2004, available from *www.brookings.edu/fp/cnaps/ papers/yamaji2004.pdf.*

Yun, Philip W. and Gi-Wook Shin, *North Korea: 2005 and Beyond*, Stanford, CA: The Walter H. Shorenstein Asia-Pacific Research Center, 2006.

Zilian, Frederick, *From Confrontation to Cooperation: The Takeover of the National People's (East German) Army by the Bundeswehr*, Praeger Studies in Diplomacy and Strategic Thought, Westport, CT: Praeger, 1999.